COUNTRY PROFILE: UNITED ARAB EMIRATES (UAE)

July 2007

COUNTRY PROFILE: UNITED ARAB EMIRATES (UAE)

July 2007

COUNTRY

Formal Name: United Arab Emirates (Al Imarat al Arabiyah al Muttahidah) الـعـربـيّـة الـمـتّـحدة. الإمارات The seven emirates, in order of size, are: Abu Dhabi (Abu Zaby) أبو ظـبـي, Dubai (Dubayy) دبـيّ, Sharjah (Ash Shariqah) الشــارقة, Umm al Qaywayn أمّ الـقـيويـن, Al Ajman عجمان, Al Fajayrah الـفجـيـرة, and Ras al Khaymah رأس الخـيمة.

Short Form: UAE.

Term for Citizen(s): Emirati(s). امراتى

Capital: Abu Dhabi City. أبو ظـبـي

Major Cities: Al Ayn, capital of the Eastern Region, and Madinat Zayid, capital of the Western Region, are located in Abu Dhabi Emirate, the largest and most populous emirate. Dubai City is located in Dubai Emirate, the second largest emirate. Sharjah City and Khawr Fakkan are the major cities of the third largest emirate—Sharjah.

Independence: The United Kingdom announced in 1968 and reaffirmed in 1971 that it would end its treaty relationships with the seven Trucial Coast states, which had been under British protection since 1892. Following the termination of all existing treaties with Britain, on December 2, 1971, six of the seven sheikhdoms formed the United Arab Emirates (UAE). The seventh sheikhdom, Ras al Khaymah, joined the UAE in 1972.

Public holidays: Public holidays other than New Year's Day and UAE National Day are dependent on the Islamic calendar and vary from year to year. For 2007, the holidays are: New Year's Day (January 1); Muharram, Islamic New Year (January 20); Mouloud, Birth of Muhammad (March 31); Accession of the Ruler of Abu Dhabi—observed only in Abu Dhabi (August 6); Leilat al Meiraj, Ascension of Muhammad (August 10); first day of Ramadan (September 13); Eid al Fitr, end of Ramadan (October 13); UAE National Day (December 2); Eid al Adha, Feast of the Sacrifice (December 20); and Christmas Day (December 25).

Flag: The UAE flag has three equal horizontal bands of green (on top), white, and black, with a wider vertical red band on the hoist side.

Click to Enlarge Image

HISTORICAL BACKGROUND

Early Years: The United Arab Emirates (UAE) was formed from the group of tribally organized Arabian Peninsula sheikhdoms along the southern coast of the Persian Gulf and the northwestern coast of the Gulf of Oman. This area was converted to Islam in the seventh century and for centuries afterward was embroiled in dynastic disputes. Most UAE nationals are descended from two tribal groupings, the Qawasim and the Bani Yas, which emerged as leading powers in the eighteenth century. The Qawasim, mainly land and sea traders, dominated what are today the emirates of Ras al Khaymah and Sharjah. The Bani Yas, who were agricultural and pastoral, lived in what are today the emirates of Abu Dhabi and Dubai. From the seventeenth to the nineteenth century, the area became known as the Pirate Coast, as both European and Arab pirates attacked foreign ships. The British mounted expeditions against the pirates during this period, culminating in an 1818 campaign against the pirate headquarters of Ras al Khaymah and other harbors along the coast. This action ostensibly was taken to safeguard British maritime routes, particularly those of the British East India Company, but some historians have noted that the war was in fact motivated by the British desire to establish supremacy in the region against the claims of other European powers.

British Rule: In 1820 Britain concluded a general treaty of peace with the principal sheikhs of the Pirate Coast and Bahrain. Its purpose was to end plundering and piracy and to establish a commitment to desist from the slave trade. The 1820 treaty includes the first denunciation of the slave trade ever written into a formal treaty. However, this treaty did not in practice prevent regular warfare at sea among the tribes of the coast, and in 1835 the sheikhs agreed to a new truce, pursuant to which they agreed to report aggression to British political or naval authorities rather than to retaliate themselves. This truce was renewed several times until May 1853, with the signing of a treaty to bring a complete halt to all hostilities at sea, establishing a "perpetual maritime truce." The truce was supervised by Britain, to whom the signatories referred all violations. The coastal sheikhdoms now became known as the Trucial Coast, stemming from the treaties signed with the British that resulted in the maritime truce, or as Trucial Oman, because the treaties separated the sheikhdoms from Oman. These terms remained in use until 1971, upon independence from Britain.

In 1892, as France, Germany, and Russia were developing an interest in the Gulf Region, Britain and the sheikhs of the Trucial Coast signed a new treaty, known as the "Exclusive Agreement." Under this treaty, the sheikhs agreed not to enter into any agreement or correspondence with any power other than Britain and not to cede, sell, or mortgage any part of their territory to anyone other than Britain without British consent. From this period until independence in 1971, the individual coastal sheikhdoms were under British protection, which meant that Britain assumed responsibility for their defense and external relations, while the sheikhdoms followed the traditional form of Arab monarchy, i.e., each ruler had virtually absolute power over his subjects.

Road to Independence: In 1952 Britain recommended that the rulers of the seven sheihkdoms establish the Trucial Council to encourage the adoption of common policies in administrative matters, possibly leading to a federation of states. The rulers met at least twice a year under the chairmanship of the political agent in Dubai.

Since 1958, when petroleum was first discovered beneath the coastal waters of Abu Dhabi, petroleum assets have largely determined the power structure and relative prestige of the emirates. Onshore petroleum was found in Abu Dhabi in 1960, and commercial production followed in 1962, providing significant wealth to the sheikhdom, which remains the largest and most affluent emirate. Sheikh Shakhbut ibn Sultan Al Nuhayyan, who had ruled Abu Dhabi since

1928, failed to use the income from petroleum royalties to develop the sheikhdom and was deposed in 1966. He was replaced by his younger brother, Sheikh Zayid ibn Sultan Al Nuhayyan, under whose rule Abu Dhabi was transformed, with considerable income from the petroleum industry allocated for public works and the provision of welfare services. In 1966 petroleum was discovered in Dubai, which prospered greatly from this new wealth.

Independence: In 1968 the United Kingdom announced its decision, reaffirmed in March 1971, to end the treaty relationships with the seven Trucial Coast states and to withdraw British military forces from the area. In March 1968, the Trucial Coast states joined Bahrain and Qatar (which had also been under British protection) to form the Federation of Arab Emirates, but Bahrain and Qatar seceded from the federation in 1971, opting for separate independence. In July 1971, six of the Trucial States (Abu Dhabi, Ajman, Al Fujayrah, Dubai, Sharjah, and Umm al Qaywayn) agreed on a federal constitution for achieving independence as the United Arab Emirates (UAE). On December 1, 1971, the United Kingdom terminated all existing treaties with the Trucial Coast states, and independence was declared the following day. The seventh sheikhdom, Ras al Khaymah, joined the UAE in February 1972. At the time of independence, Sheikh Zayid ibn Sultan Al Nuhayyan of Abu Dhabi was named the first president of the UAE, a role he fulfilled until his death in 2004. The ruler of Dubai, Sheikh Rashid ibn Said Al Maktum, became vice president, and his eldest son, Sheikh Maktum ibn Rashid Al Maktum, the crown prince of Dubai, was named prime minister. In 1986 Sheikh Rashid assumed the posts of both vice president and prime minister, but on his death in 1990 Sheikh Maktum succeeded his father as ruler of Dubai and as vice president and prime minister of the UAE.

In 1971 the UAE adopted a provisional constitution that was intended to expire after five years but it was in fact renewed until the adoption of a permanent constitution in 1996. The government was centralized further in 1976, when the federal government attained control over defense, intelligence services, immigration, public security, and border control.

GEOGRAPHY

Location: The UAE is situated on the Arabian Peninsula between Oman and Saudi Arabia and bordering the Gulf of Oman and the Persian Gulf.

Click to Enlarge Image

Size: The UAE government estimates the total area of the UAE to be 83,600 square kilometers; excluding the three islands in the Strait of Hormuz, the area is 77,700 square kilometers (slightly smaller than the state of Maine). Abu Dhabi has an area of 67,350 square kilometers.

Land Boundaries: The UAE's land boundaries total 867 kilometers. The emirates border Oman to the north and east (410 kilometers) and Saudi Arabia to the west and south (457 kilometers).

Disputed Territory: In 1974 Abu Dhabi and Saudi Arabia reached agreement settling a dispute over the Al Buraymi Oasis and other territory to the south, but the agreement has not been ratified by the UAE or recognized by Saudi Arabia. The UAE signed and ratified a boundary agreement with Oman in 2003 for the entire border, including Oman's Musandam Peninsula and Al Madhah enclaves, but the agreement and accompanying maps have not been made public. In 1992 Iran unilaterally took full control over three islands in the Strait of Hormuz—Greater and Lesser Tunb and Abu Musa, which it had shared with the Sharjah Emirate since 1971. At their annual summit in December 2006, Gulf Cooperation Council (GCC) leaders reiterated their unequivocal support for UAE sovereignty over the three islands and urged Iran, which has expanded its civilian and military presence on all three disputed islands, to respond to efforts for a peaceful settlement, either through direct negotiations or by referring the issue to the International Court of Justice. In February 2007, the 22-member Council of Arab Parliamentary Union also reaffirmed the UAE's sovereignty over the three islands.

Length of Coastline: The UAE has 1,318 kilometers of coastline along the Persian Gulf and Gulf of Oman.

Maritime Claims: The UAE claims a territorial sea of 12 nautical miles, a contiguous zone of 24 nautical miles, an exclusive economic zone of 200 nautical miles, and a continental shelf of 200 nautical miles or to the edge of the continental margin.

Topography: The UAE is primarily flat or rolling desert. Its coast, which stretches along the southern shore of the Persian Gulf, consists mainly of salt pans that extend far inland. The largest natural harbor is Dubai. The UAE also extends for about 90 kilometers along the Gulf of Oman, an area known as the Al Batinah coast. The UAE's highest point, at 1,527 meters, is Jabal Yibir in the jagged Al Hajar al Gharbi mountain chain, which splits the UAE from north to south in the northern emirates. Beginning at the UAE–Oman border on the Persian Gulf coast of the Musandam Peninsula, the mountains extend southeastward for approximately 150 kilometers to the southernmost UAE–Oman border on the Gulf of Oman. The mountain slopes tend to run right to the shore, except in the vicinity of Al Fujayrah, where there are sandy beaches. South and west of Abu Dhabi, vast, rolling sand dunes merge into the Rub al Khali of Saudi Arabia.

Principal Rivers: The UAE has no permanent rivers, but the desert area of Abu Dhabi includes two important oases with adequate underground water for permanent settlements and cultivation. The extensive Al Liwa Oasis is in the south near the undefined border with Saudi Arabia. Approximately 200 kilometers to the northeast of the Al Liwa Oasis is the Al Buraymi Oasis, which extends on both sides of the Abu Dhabi–Oman border.

Climate: The climate of the UAE is generally hot and dry. The summer months (July and August) are the hottest, with temperatures exceeding 40° C, coupled with very high humidity. The average temperature in the winter months, January and February, is 17° C–20° C. In the Al Hajar al Gharbi Mountains, temperatures are much cooler as a result of the increased elevation. The average annual rainfall in the coastal area is very low—between 100 millimeters and 200 millimeters—but in some mountainous areas annual rainfall reaches 350 millimeters. Rain in the coastal region falls in short, torrential bursts during the summer months.

Natural Resources: Oil and natural gas are the primary natural resources in the UAE, and petroleum production is the most important industry.

Land Use: Only 0.6 percent of the UAE is considered to be arable land, and 2.3 percent of the land is planted to permanent crops. About 720 square kilometers of land are irrigated.

Environmental Factors: The UAE is subject to frequent sand and dust storms, which can severely reduce visibility. The smaller islands in the Persian Gulf, as well as many coral reefs and shifting sandbars, are a menace to navigation. Strong tides and occasional windstorms further complicate ship movements near the shore. Desalinization plants compensate for the lack of freshwater resources, but desertification (land degradation caused by aridity) and beach pollution from oil spills are serious problems.

Time Zone: The UAE is four hours ahead of Greenwich Mean Time.

SOCIETY

Population: According to the official census conducted in 2005, estimates for the UAE's population for that year range from 4.1 million to 4.6 million; the population is estimated to increase to 4.9 million in 2006. The overall population increased by almost 75 percent from 1995 to 2005, with the percentage of non-nationals increasing at a much faster rate than the national population. The current annual growth rate is estimated at 6.9 percent. The majority of the population (2.5 million) is urban and lives in the two largest emirates—Abu Dhabi and Dubai. Dubai has the fastest growing population, with an average annual growth rate of 8.5 percent between the years 2000 and 2005.

Demography: The UAE's population is predominantly young. According to U.S. government estimates based on a total population of 4.4 million, more than 75 percent of the population (about 3.4 million) is 15 to 64 years of age, roughly 20 percent (about 900,000) is less than 14 years of age, and less than 1 percent (about 38,000) is 65 and older. The population is male dominant, with males numbering 3 million and females, 1.4 million. In 2007 the birthrate and death rate are estimated to be 16.1 per 1,000 and 2.2 per 1,000, respectively. The infant mortality rate, like the population, is estimated to be higher for males—nearly 16 deaths per 1,000 live births, as compared with about 13 female deaths per 1,000 live births. The UAE has a relatively high level of life expectancy: 73.2 years for males and nearly 78.4 years for females, or 75.7 years overall. The country's fertility rate is greater than 2.4 children per woman.

Ethnic Groups and Languages: UAE citizens constitute approximately 20 percent of the population. The rest are foreign workers, predominantly from South and Southeast Asia (approximately 60 percent of the population). The remainder of the expatriate population includes a significant number of other Arabs—Palestinians, Egyptians, Jordanians, Yemenis, and Omanis—as well as many Iranians, Pakistanis, Indians, Bangladeshis, Afghanis, Filipinos, and West Europeans. Arabic is the official language. Other languages spoken include Persian, English, Hindi, Persian, and Urdu. English is widely understood in the UAE.

Religion: The vast majority (approximately 96 percent) of the UAE's citizens are Muslims; approximately 85 percent of Muslims are Sunni and 15 percent, Shia. The government funds or subsidizes almost 95 percent of Sunni mosques and employs all Sunni imams. A central federal regulatory authority distributes weekly guidance to both Sunni imams and Shia sheikhs regarding the content of sermons.

The UAE's constitution declares that Islam is the official religion of all seven of the constituent emirates of the federal union. Muslims are expressly prohibited from converting to other religions, but conversion by non-Muslims to Islam is viewed favorably. During Ramadan, all residents and visitors are required to abide by restrictions imposed on Muslims. Islamic studies are mandatory for citizen children attending public schools and for Muslim children attending private schools. Religious instruction in non-Muslim religions is not permitted in public schools.

According to the U.S. Department of State, non-Muslim religious leaders within the UAE and outside the country regard the UAE as one of the most liberal and broad-minded countries in the region in terms of governmental and societal attitudes toward other faiths. The UAE government generally follows a policy of tolerance toward non-Muslim religions and, in practice, does not interfere very much with their religious activities. However, the government does prohibit non-Muslims from proselytizing or distributing religious literature under penalty of criminal prosecution, imprisonment, or deportation, deeming such behavior to be offensive to Islam. In 2006 numerous meetings and dialogue conferences were held between UAE religious and political leaders and representatives of non-Muslim countries and churches to discuss religious tolerance.

Education and Literacy: According to the UAE government, the overall literacy rate is 91 percent. The government has set a goal of achieving full literacy before 2010.

The UAE currently devotes approximately 25 percent of total federal government spending to education. Public education is free for male and female citizen children through the university level. Beginning in the academic year 2006–7, expatriate students may, for a fee, attend government schools. The UAE has one of the lowest pupil-to-teacher ratios (15:1) in the world. Education is compulsory through the ninth grade, although, according to the U.S. Department of State, this requirement is not enforced. Citizen children are required to attend gender-segregated schools through the sixth grade, the last grade of primary education. In 2004–5 approximately 9.9 percent of students in grades one through five and 8.3 percent of students in grades six through nine did not complete their education; this rate rose to 9.3 percent in grades 10–12.

The Ministry of Education has adopted "Education 2020," a series of five-year plans designed to introduce advanced education techniques, improve innovative skills, and focus more on the self-learning abilities of students. As part of this program, an enhanced curriculum for mathematics and integrated science was introduced at first-grade level for the 2003–4 academic year in all government schools. In addition, the UAE government believes that a poor grasp of English is one of the main employment barriers for UAE nationals; as a first remedial step, the Abu Dhabi Education Council is developing an elementary school pilot program with Zayid University, which it hopes to extend to all schools in the emirate, to enhance student English language skills. In February 2006, the prime minister directed the education minister to take initial steps toward improving the quality of education, including the provision of permanent classrooms, computer laboratories, and modern facilities. In April 2007, however, in a major policy speech to the nation, the UAE vice president and prime minister stated that despite the steady increase in the education budget over the previous 20 years, teaching methods and curricula were obsolete, and the education system as a whole was weak. He demanded that the ministers of education and higher education work to find innovative and comprehensive solutions.

At the higher education level, numerous institutions are available to the student body. In 1976 UAE University (UAEU) was established in Al Ayn in Abu Dhabi. Consisting of nine colleges, it is considered by the UAE government to be the leading teaching and research institution in the country. More than 14,000 students were enrolled at UAEU in the first semester of the academic year 2006–7. In 1988 the first four Higher Colleges of Technology (HCT) were opened. In the academic year 2005–6, 12 campuses offered more than 75 programs, with a combined enrollment of 15,000 men and women. The commercial arm of the HCT, the Centre of Excellence for Applied Research and Training, is allied with multinational companies to provide training courses and professional development. In 1998 Zayid University was opened for women with campuses in Abu Dhabi and Dubai. A new US$100.7 million campus in Dubai opened in 2006.

In 2003 Dubai established a dedicated education zone, Knowledge Village, based at Dubai Internet City, to bring together globally recognized international universities, training centers, e-learning, and research and development companies in one location. As of early 2007, it had attracted 16 international university partners. In October 2006, France's Sorbonne opened a campus in Abu Dhabi.

Health: Standards of health care are considered to be generally high in the UAE, resulting from increased government spending during strong economic years. According to the UAE government, total expenditures on health care from 1996 to 2003 were US$436 million. According to the World Health Organization, in 2004 total expenditures on health care constituted 2.9 percent of gross domestic product (GDP), and the per capita expenditure for health care was US$497. Health care currently is free only for UAE citizens. Effective January 2006, all residents of Abu Dhabi are covered by a new comprehensive health insurance program; costs will be shared between employers and employees. The number of doctors per 100,000 (annual average, 1990–99) is 181. The UAE now has 40 public hospitals, compared with only seven in 1970. The Ministry of Health is undertaking a multimillion-dollar program to expand health facilities—hospitals, medical centers, and a trauma center—in the seven emirates. A state-of-the-art general hospital has opened in Abu Dhabi with a projected bed capacity of 143, a trauma unit, and the first home health care program in the UAE. To attract wealthy UAE nationals and expatriates who traditionally have traveled abroad for serious medical care, Dubai is developing Dubai Healthcare City, a hospital free zone that will offer international-standard advanced private health care and provide an academic medical training center; completion is scheduled for 2010.

Cardiovascular disease is the principal cause of death in the UAE, constituting 28 percent of total deaths; other major causes are accidents and injuries, malignancies, and congenital anomalies. In 1985 the UAE established a national program to prevent transmission of acquired immune deficiency syndrome (AIDS) and to control its entry into the country. According to World Health Organization estimates, in 2002–3 fewer than 1,000 people in the UAE were living with human immunodeficiency virus (HIV)/AIDS.

Welfare: Among developing nations, as categorized by the United Nations, the UAE ranks 49 out of 177 countries on the human development index, a measure of life expectancy, education, and standard of living. In 1999 the Federal National Council approved legislation providing monthly social security benefits to national widows and divorced women, the disabled and handicapped, the aged, orphans, single daughters, married students, relatives of jailed dependents, estranged wives, and insolvents. Also eligible are widowed and divorced national women previously married to foreigners and expatriate husbands of UAE national women. The recipient population dropped between 1980 and 2005, but the cost to the government rose as a result of a higher cost of living. In October 2005, welfare payments to UAE nationals, including the unemployed, increased by 75 percent. As a result, annual social allocations to a beneficiary population of more than 67,000 rose from approximately US$179.2 million to approximately US$309.1 million. Social security entitlements constitute 1–2 percent of gross domestic product.

ECONOMY

Overview: In the 40 years since oil was first discovered and exported, the UAE has been transformed from a region of small sheikhdoms subsisting on pearling, fishing, herding, and agriculture to a modern state with a high per capita income and substantial trade surplus. The largest and wealthiest emirate is Abu Dhabi, which is the principal petroleum producer and financier of the federation. Dubai, the second largest emirate, thrives on wealth derived from a services-based economy (tourism, construction, telecommunications, media, real estate, and financial services). Together, the two emirates provide more than 80 percent of the UAE's income, while the northern emirates remain relatively undeveloped. Key economic policy decisions are made at the emirate level with little coordination among the seven emirates.

The UAE economy remains heavily dependent on oil and natural gas; the revenue from oil exports in particular enables the government to finance infrastructure for the non-oil economy. Economists forecast that in 2007–8 the economy is expected to grow at an average annual rate of approximately 7 percent. Investment in manufacturing and energy-intensive sectors such as petrochemicals and metals will drive the non-oil sector, aided by exports made more competitive by the weakness of the U.S. dollar. The services sector, primarily tourism, is expected to continue to gain strength.

Sheikh Khalifa ibn Zayid Al Nuhayyan, who succeeded his father as president of the UAE in November 2004, is expected to continue the relatively liberal economic policies of his predecessor: privatization of some government assets; provision of incentives for foreign and domestic private investment; avoidance of a national income or sales tax; and curtailment of both money laundering and the use of the banking system to foster terrorist activities.

In April 2007, vice president and prime minister Sheikh Mohammed ibn Rashid Al Maktum delivered a major policy speech in which he outlined a comprehensive three-year UAE Government Strategy, the core of which is sustainable economic development. He placed heavy emphasis on upgrading the UAE's education system and making emiratisation a national priority.

Gross Domestic Product (GDP): In 2004 the UAE's GDP was US$105.2 billion. Economists calculate the 2005 real GDP growth rate at 8.2 percent, with GDP exceeding US$132 billion. Per capita GDP for 2005 was high compared with other Arab countries—almost US$29,000. For the period 2006–7, real GDP growth is expected to remain strong, driven not only by high oil earnings but also by sustained expansion in the non-oil sectors. Real GDP is forecast to grow 8.9 percent in 2006, with GDP exceeding US$162 billion, and to grow 7 percent in 2007.

Government Budget: The UAE federal budget accounts for approximately 25 percent of total federation fiscal transactions; the remainder consists of the fiscal operations of the individual emirates, and the combined expenditures constitute the consolidated accounts. Oil revenue accounts for more than 60 percent of all income, and consequently the volatility of the oil market has created significant fluctuations in government income. Economists calculate that based on rising global oil prices offset by significant public-sector pay increases and higher capital expenditures, the 2004 budget ran a relatively small deficit of US$233 million (0.2 percent of gross domestic product (GDP), as compared with deficits in 2002 and 2003 that were 11 percent and 4.5 percent of GDP, respectively). According to the UAE government, in 2005 a 20-year period of fiscal deficits came to a close when the government budget had a surplus of approximately US$10.4 billion (almost 8 percent of GDP), as revenues increased by 70 percent, and expenditures, fueled by large increases in public-sector wages, rose by 27 percent.

In 2006, as a result of rising oil prices and increased production, the budget is expected to generate an estimated US$20 billion surplus (approximately 12.4 percent of GDP). The surplus is expected to decline to 8.4 percent and 7.4 percent of GDP in 2007 and 2008, respectively, as a result of expenditure growth outpacing revenue growth. However, economists caution that UAE fiscal data inaccurately reflect the actual strength of the government's finances, for two reasons. First, a significant portion of Abu Dhabi's oil earnings are not reported as current revenue, but rather are paid directly into reserve accounts. Second, the data do not reflect the substantial income generated by the emirates from overseas investments (estimated in 2006 to be more than US$600 billion), most of which are held by Abu Dhabi. Both of these revenue streams fund part of the federal deficit; were they to be factored into the budget equation, the government budget would actually show no deficit in 2004 and a higher surplus in ensuing years.

Inflation: Inflation in the UAE is more marked than in most of the oil-based Gulf economies and has risen sharply in the past two years, reaching approximately 6 percent in 2005 according to UAE government figures. This rise is attributed to a surge in domestic demand generated by escalating housing prices and service-sector costs, which in turn have driven up wage demands in the private sector. As a counter measure, the government of Dubai has banned any increases in rents (with limited exceptions) for 2007, and the government of Abu Dhabi has capped 2007 rent increases at 7 percent. Economists note, however, that UAE government inflation data reflect only costs incurred by UAE nationals, who constitute only one-fifth of the population and are protected by an extensive system of subsidies that restrict price increases on a range of core goods and services. A more realistic measure of the cost of living for all UAE residents (factoring in the weakening of the dirham against the dollar) would result in an inflation rate close to 12.5 percent in 2005, 13.5 percent in 2006, and an estimated 9 percent in 2007 and 7 percent in 2008.

Agriculture, Forestry, and Fishing: As a result of adverse climatic conditions (nutrient-poor soil, extreme aridity, and high summer temperatures) in the UAE, in 2005 agriculture represented a relatively small portion (an estimated 3 percent) of the country's gross domestic product. Employment in the agricultural sector occupied only approximately 7 percent of the employed population in 2005, but because a relatively high proportion of UAE nationals are employed in farming, the sector receives a disproportionate share of government subsidies at both the federal and local levels. Dates remain the UAE's major crop in terms of area cultivated, but the production of vegetables has increased dramatically, particularly in Abu Dhabi, and currently generates the most revenue. Other major products are eggs, dairy products, and poultry.

Fishing and pearl diving traditionally were an important part of the economy, but the pearl industry collapsed with the development of cultured pearls. Fishing is done almost exclusively for domestic consumption. There is no fish-processing industry in the UAE to provide a market for the 20,000 or more tons of fish caught each year that exceed local demand, and the surplus is either exported or returned to the sea.

Mining and Minerals: The UAE's economy is dominated by the oil and gas sector, which accounts for more than 30 percent of total gross domestic product. The Supreme Petroleum Council, headed by the crown prince of Abu Dhabi, has ultimate control over energy policy in the UAE. Despite the crown prince's commitment to diversifying the economy by reducing dependency on oil, the UAE government is investing billions of dollars to increase crude oil capacity from approximately 2.7 million barrels per day in 2006 to 4 million barrels per day by 2010.

According to statistics published in June 2006, the UAE contains proven crude oil reserves of 98 billion barrels, or almost 8 percent of the world total. Of this amount, Abu Dhabi holds 94 percent (approximately 92.2 billion barrels). Dubai contains approximately 4.0 billion barrels. Under the UAE's constitution, each emirate controls its own production and resource development. Abu Dhabi became a member of the Organization of the Petroleum Exporting Countries (OPEC) in 1967, but Dubai does not consider itself part of OPEC or bound by its quotas. In October 2006, the UAE became a signatory to an OPEC agreement to reduce oil production by 1.2 million barrels per day, which would result in a reduction of UAE output of 101,000 barrels per day. According to International Energy Agency statistics, the UAE's crude oil production in the fourth quarter of 2006 was 2.6 million barrels per day, which is 50,000 barrels per day lower than during the previous quarter; production fell slightly to 2.57 million barrels per day in first quarter of 2007.

According to statistics published in January 2006, the UAE has natural gas reserves of 214.4 trillion cubic feet, the fifth largest supply in the world after Russia, Iran, Qatar, and Saudi Arabia. Abu Dhabi holds the largest reserves—198.5 trillion cubic feet. The emirates of Sharjah, Dubai, and Ras al Khaymah hold considerably smaller reserves. In the past 10 years, natural gas consumption in Abu Dhabi has doubled to a current rate of approximately 4 billion cubic feet per day.

Industry and Manufacturing: Industry (including mining, manufacturing, construction, and power) accounted for an estimated 54.2 percent of the gross domestic product (GDP) in 2005 and employed almost 36 percent of the workforce in that year. The major heavy industries in the UAE are related to oil and gas, and the bulk of the manufacturing industry is centered in the Jabal Ali Free Zone in Dubai and the Jabal az Zannah-Ar Ruways industrial zone in Abu Dhabi. The main products are liquefied petroleum gas, distillate fuel oils, and jet fuels. Manufacturing constituted 12.9 percent of GDP in 2004 and employed 13 percent of the workforce in that year. Aluminum has emerged as a key manufacturing activity over the last 20 years as a result of the growth of Dubai Aluminum, owned by the Dubai government. The company's 2006 production capacity of 850,000 tons per year placed it as one of the world's top 10 producers. In mid-2006, Dubai and a company owned by the Abu Dhabi government signed an agreement to establish a smelter in Abu Dhabi with a capacity of 1.2 million tons per year; the first phase is scheduled to be operational in 2010. Other manufacturing sub-sectors are steel and chemicals.

Energy: In 1997, in response to the UAE's rising demand for electric power, coupled with volatile swings in peak loads, the Abu Dhabi government formed the Privatization Committee for the Water and Electricity Sector to assess the emirate's energy requirements and consider privatization as an option. This committee recommended that Abu Dhabi's water and electricity department be changed to a semi-autonomous regulatory body, the Abu Dhabi Water and Electricity Authority (ADWEA), and that the emirate's power stations be partially or totally privatized. The privatization of production through the creation of independent water and power projects (IWPPs) has become the cornerstone of ADWEA's strategy to meet continuing increased demand for power and water (estimated to rise 10 to 15 percent a year). As of 2005, there were six major IWPPs in Abu Dhabi.

The first IWPP was the US$800 million Taweelah A–2 project, which became fully operational in 2001 and added 763 megawatts of power and 50 million gallons per day of desalinated water to the UAE's supplies. As in all IWPP joint ventures, ADWEA has a 60 percent share in the company established to build, own, and operate the plant; the remaining 40 percent is owned by overseas private investors. Taweelah A–1, a project expanding an existing facility to bring capacity to 1,350 megawatts and 84 million gallons per day, was completed in May 2003. The Taweelah B plant, where capacity is currently 1,070 megawatts and 90 million gallons per day, is slated for a US$3 billion expansion. An international consortium has completed an agreement with ADWEA; by 2008 power capacity will be increased to 2,115 megawatts and water desalination capacity raised by 65 million gallons per day.

Estimated to cost US$8 to US$10 billion over the next decade, the Dolphin gas pipeline project was formulated in 1999 to bring gas from Qatar's massive offshore North Dome Field to the UAE via a 370-kilometer offshore export pipeline. Despite construction delays and jurisdictional objections from Saudi Arabia in mid-2006, the gas came on stream in March 2007 with initial flows of 200 million cubic feet per day. Full initial capacity of 2 billion cubic feet per day is expected by late 2007 or early 2008. Although the pipeline was built to carry a full capacity of 3.2 billion cubic feet per day, in February 2007 the Qatar government stated that Qatar would not be able to supply the additional 1.2 billion cubic feet per day. This project is important to the UAE's northern emirates, especially Dubai, where natural gas resources are not meeting demand. In addition, the pipeline is viewed as a long-term solution to the rising demand for power and water, because natural gas is the primary fuel for power generation and desalinization plants.

The UAE is positioning itself strategically in the Gulf region by participating in a US$1 billion project to build a regional power grid throughout the Gulf Cooperation Council countries. The first phase links Saudi Arabia, Bahrain, and Qatar. The UAE and Oman would participate in the second phase, contingent on each country's having its own unified power grid. In 2003 the UAE awarded a contract to Electricité de France to connect all the power stations along its western coast with the central region.

Services: According to the UAE government, the services sector (including financial enterprises and government services) produced 43.1 percent of the gross domestic product (GDP) in 2004 and 40.4 percent of GDP in 2005. This sector employed more than 1.4 million persons in 2004 and almost 1.5 million in 2005, which is approximately 60 percent of the total workforce.

Banking and Finance: The UAE Central Bank was established in 1980 to direct monetary, credit, and banking policy. It maintains the UAE government's reserves of gold and foreign currencies, acts as the bank for banks operating in the UAE, and serves as the state's financial agent at international financial institutions. In response to pressure from the World Trade Organization to open the banking sector to more foreign competition, in late 2004 the UAE Central Bank stated that it would consider allowing new foreign banks to establish themselves in the UAE for the first time in 20 years. As of late 2006, however, no new licenses had been issued. Relative to its population and gross domestic product, the UAE has an unusually high number of banks—21 local, 25 foreign, 2 specialized, and approximately 50 representative offices of other foreign banks. The top six commercial banks control 70 percent of total banking assets and reported very strong profit growth from 2002 through 2005. Although the sharp drop in prices on the UAE stock markets negatively affected bank profits, in 2006 the sector remained profitable overall, primarily as a result of the growth of conventional retail and commercial banking (personal loans, credit cards, and residential mortgages).

The Dubai International Financial Center (DIFC) opened officially in September 2004. The DIFC is a self-regulating financial free zone, operated independently of the UAE Central Bank and including more than a dozen international financial institutions. In September 2005, it established the Dubai International Financial Exchange, which provides markets for equities, bonds, funds, sharia-compliant products, and derivatives and is fully open to foreign investment.

The Dubai Financial Market (DFM) and the Abu Dhabi Securities Market opened in March 2000 and have been linked electronically since 2004. Both stock markets surged in value and liquidity from 2002 until November 2005, when a steep decline began that did not reverse until early 2007. The sharp downturn in stock prices in 2006 was Gulf-wide and is attributed to the overvaluation of stocks and heavy bank borrowing to finance initial public offerings.

Islamic banking has assumed a more prominent role in the UAE in recent years, and most conventional banks are opening or expanding Islamic banking departments; sharia-compliant consumer and investment products also are being introduced. Government agencies and majority state-owned companies are using Islamic bonds—*sukuk*—to finance development and acquisitions.

Terrorism is financed using the banking system in two primary ways—through money laundering and through financial transactions in the *hawala* system, which is a traditional alternative remittance system that operates outside the control of the conventional banking sector. After 9/11 a link was drawn between branches of Citibank in the UAE and the United States and financing of the terrorist attacks. In response, the UAE Central Bank has frozen the assets of organizations suspected of having ties to al Qaeda or to the former Taliban regime in Afghanistan and educates financial institutions on countering money laundering and terrorist financing . Legislation was enacted in 2002 tightening reporting requirements for financial transactions and increasing penalties for money laundering. *Hawala* operators, thought to be the conduit for much of the funding earmarked for terrorist activities, are now licensed in the UAE and required to report suspicious transactions to the UAE government. As of early 2007, the UAE Central Bank had registered 201 *hawala* dealers.

Tourism: The primary source of the UAE's rapidly growing tourism sector is the Dubai Emirate, which hosts the world's tallest hotel. According to the UAE government, Dubai's tourism revenue exceeds its oil revenue. The emirate's 302 hotels hosted 6.4 million visitors from India, Pakistan, Iran, Lebanon, the Philippines, Europe, Australia, and South Africa in 2006. However, according to the UAE government, the emirate's initial target of 15 million visitors by 2010 will not be met because of airport and hotel construction delays, coupled with delays in obtaining additional aircraft for the major carrier, Emirates. The main attractions for tourists are beaches, nightlife, shopping, and luxurious accommodations. Dubai has grandiose plans for the future—the building of four man-made island structures off the coast (valued at US$3 billion each), which will house more than 100 new hotels, and the US$9.5 billion theme park Dubailand, which will include a cluster of 31 new hotels.

Abu Dhabi hosted 1.2 million tourists in 2005 and has targeted 3 million hotel guests per year by 2015. Numerous luxury hotel projects and a new cultural district, the centerpiece of which will be a branch of the Louvre Museum, are under development.

Labor: Numerous labor issues plague the UAE, resulting directly from the disproportionate number of expatriates (80 percent of the population) living and working there. In 2004 expatriates constituted 2.5 million of the total labor force of 2.7 million, which means that nationals constituted less than 10 percent of the employed population. Nationals make up an estimated 80 percent of the federal and emirate-level civil service but hold only 2 percent of jobs in the private sector, which provides 52 percent of the jobs in the UAE. In April 2007, the UAE government unveiled a new national strategy that declared "emiratisation" of the workforce to be at the heart of the country's future economic development. In recent years, the government has explored various ways to create employment opportunities for UAE nationals in several economic sectors. In June 2006, a government decree mandated the replacement of all private-sector expatriate secretaries and human resources managers with UAE nationals. In February 2007, the government posted online for comment the draft of a new labor law that would impose a minimum quota of UAE nationals across the private sector.

More than 500,000 low-skilled, poorly paid (often unpaid) South Asians work in the UAE in substandard living conditions without any rights or recourse for alleged abuses. Workers reportedly are denied health care, and there have been numerous instances of industrial accidents, some fatal, particularly in the construction industry, which is the main employer of expatriate Asian labor. Numerous publicized worker demonstrations and other negative publicity, including November 2006 and January 2007 reports by the U.S.-based nongovernmental organization Human Rights Watch and the United Nations High Commissioner for Refugees, respectively, charging that the UAE had failed to prevent the abuse of the country's migrant construction workers, have evoked some response from the UAE government. The Ministry of Labor has negotiated some worker benefits with employers and begun construction of new housing outside Abu Dhabi for foreign workers. In addition, the UAE labor minister has met with representatives of India, Pakistan, Sri Lanka, Bangladesh, China, the Philippines, Indonesia, and Nepal to advise them of remedial measures the UAE will take to ensure better and safer living and working conditions for workers from their countries. At the same time, however, the Ministry of Labor is beginning to enforce a September 2006 law banning strikes and has vowed to deport foreign workers participating in protests that are not triggered by employment contract violations. In March 2007, the government deported dozens of striking South Asian workers in Dubai.

Confirming his pledge on taking office to promote the interests of UAE nationals, in early 2005 the UAE president announced a 25 percent pay increase for all citizens working in federal government institutions as well as the UAE armed forces and employees of the Abu Dhabi Emirate, effective May 1, 2005. Expatriates working in the public sector were eligible for a 15-percent raise. In February 2007, the ruler of Dubai announced a 20 percent pay increase for all national and foreign employees working in the Dubai government, retroactive to January 2007.

Foreign Economic Relations: In 1977 the Arab Monetary Fund (AMF), based in Abu Dhabi, was established by 20 Arab states to provide loans to member states, primarily for balance-of-payments support. In 1981 the UAE joined with Saudi Arabia, Kuwait, Bahrain, Qatar, and Oman to form the Gulf Cooperation Council (GCC). The UAE's closest relations within the GCC are with its major trading partner, Oman. Although the GCC was created primarily in response to regional stability and security concerns, it also serves to coordinate the economic and monetary policies of its members. The UAE is a member of the Organization of Arab Petroleum Exporting Countries, and Abu Dhabi joined the Organization of the Petroleum Exporting Countries in 1967. The UAE has been a member of the World Trade Organization (WTO) since 1996; WTO policies apply to each of the seven emirates.

In September 2003, the International Monetary Fund and World Bank held their joint annual meeting in Dubai, the first time the conference had been held in the Middle East and a clear reflection of the UAE's pro-Western stance. In March 2005, negotiations between the United States and the UAE began on a bilateral free-trade agreement (FTA). However, in March 2007 talks between the two countries, which had been derailed for several months in 2006 over the proposed Dubai Ports World purchase of U.S. port operations, were terminated, reportedly for several reasons. The United States wants greater access to the UAE's telecommunications and financial services industries, but UAE regulators of both sectors have made clear that international competition is not imminent. In addition, the UAE's restrictions on worker association, including trade unions, violate U.S. statutory requirements for FTAs.

Imports: Imports totaled US$80.2 billion in 2005 and are projected to increase to US$86 billion in 2006, US$94.6 billion in 2007, and US$104.1 billion in 2008. Principal imports are machinery and electrical equipment, precious stones and precious metals, and transport equipment. The principal source of UAE imports in 2005 was China (9.9 percent of the total). Other major countries of origin included the United Kingdom, the United States, and India.

Exports: In 2005 UAE exports totaled US$126.5 billion; this number is projected to increase to US$132.9 billion in 2006, as a result of record oil prices and the growth of non-oil exports, and to US$137.3 billion in 2007 and US$143.7 billion in 2008. According to official balance-of-payments statistics, oil and gas exports account for almost 60 percent of the UAE's total export revenues (including re-exports). Non-oil sectors of the economy contribute approximately 40 percent of the country's total exports. The primary destinations of UAE exports in 2005 were Japan (26 percent of total exports), South Korea, Thailand, and India.

Trade Balance: The UAE has recorded merchandise trade surpluses every year for more than 20 years. As a result of a small decline in international oil prices, offset by higher oil production and export volumes, economists expect continued increases in export revenues. Import spending also will continue to rise as domestic demand for capital goods to support infrastructure projects increases. The overall effect on the UAE's economy is an estimated trade surplus of nearly US$47 billion in 2006 and a projected trade surplus of more than US$41 billion in 2007 and 2008.

Balance of Payments: Economists point to two primary factors contributing to the UAE's current-account surplus: growth of services exports and greater return on the emirates' large portfolio of foreign assets. Although these inflows will be offset by higher costs associated with rising import volumes and continued reliance on foreign labor, a net current-account surplus of US$27.2 billion is calculated for 2005, and a surplus of US$25.6 billion is estimated for 2006 (about 16 percent of gross domestic product—GDP). The surplus is expected to narrow to US$20.6 billion in 2007 (about 12 percent of GDP) and to US$16.4 billion in 2008.

External Debt: The UAE does not release data on external debt, but the Organisation for Economic Co-operation and Development reported that foreign borrowing was US$18.6 billion at the end of 2000, which represented 27 percent of gross domestic product. Economists estimate that the debt stock rose to US$36.8 billion by the end of 2005. These amounts are attributed to the growing number of infrastructure projects financed through medium- and long-term foreign borrowing. According to U.S. government and International Monetary Fund estimates, UAE reserves of foreign exchange and gold in 2005 ranged from US$25 billion to US$25.5 billion.

Foreign Investment: The UAE traditionally has resisted establishing a liberal economic environment favorable to foreign investment, and each emirate retains close controls on foreign ownership rights. The country is, however, viewed as a favorable investment opportunity by regional and international firms, particularly in the energy, infrastructure, and hospitality sectors. In 2006 economists cited statistics from the United Nations Conference on Trade and Development setting the foreign direct investment (FDI) average in the UAE at only US$18 million per year from 1998 to 2002, increasing to US$8.4 billion in 2004 and to US$12 billion in

2005. According to the UAE government, which valued FDI in the UAE at US$10 billion in 2005, the UAE ranks first in the Arab world in terms of attracting inward investment.

The level of foreign investment in the UAE may increase in the near future if existing laws are liberalized. At present, the UAE's companies' law stipulates that foreign investors may own a maximum of 49 percent of a company registered in the UAE; the controlling share of the company must remain with a UAE national. Companies located in designated "free zones" may be 95 percent foreign-owned. The UAE government views the establishment of these trade zones (23 as of 2006, mostly in Dubai) as an effective magnet for foreign investment. Companies doing business there are eligible for corporate tax holidays, exemption from personal taxes, repatriation of capital and profits, and exemption from import duties and currency restrictions. The UAE government supports the introduction of a new companies' law that would allow foreigners to have a majority share, possibly 100 percent, of UAE-based firms. The government faces opposition, however, from domestic business interests in its effort to repeal the commercial agencies law, which grants UAE companies local monopolies to distribute imported goods.

In August 2005, the UAE president and ruler of Abu Dhabi issued a decree allowing non-Gulf Cooperation Council (GCC) foreigners to own property in that emirate through 99-year renewable leases on residential and commercial buildings; land ownership will remain restricted to UAE nationals. On March 14, 2006, the Dubai government issued Law No.7 allowing UAE and GCC citizens as well as expatriates to acquire freehold and 99-year lease property in designated areas in the emirate.

The Dubai International Financial Exchange, which opened at the end of September 2005, is a bond, equity, and derivatives exchange that is 100 percent open to foreign investment. The UAE wants to attract foreign issuers, particularly from the Arab world, South Africa, and India.

Foreign Aid: The Abu Dhabi Fund for Development assists developing countries in the development of their economies by extending project loans, guarantees, technical assistance grants, and equity participation. Since its founding in 1971, the fund has given between US$12 and US$15 billion in aid to more than 240 projects in 55 countries; the majority of its loan commitments (80.5 percent) have gone to Arab countries. Asian countries receive 9.5 percent of the fund's total assistance, and African countries, 7 percent.

Currency and Exchange Rate: The UAE's currency is the dirham (Dh), which is valued at Dh 3.67 per US$1. The dirham has been pegged to the U.S. dollar at this rate since the mid-1980s. In December 2001, the Gulf Cooperation Council (GCC) agreed to establish a Gulf monetary union with a single currency for the region by January 2010, but this proposal was placed in jeopardy in December 2006 when Oman withdrew support. In June 2007, the UAE Central Bank governor expressed support for an incremental monetary union implementation and indicated that the final stage, enacting uniform laws in all GCC countries, would likely be achieved after 2010.

Fiscal Year: The UAE's fiscal year coincides with the calendar year.

TRANSPORTATION AND TELECOMMUNICATIONS

Overview: The UAE's modern internal transport system was developed primarily in the 1960s and 1970s, with the construction of main roads to link the major cities. Maritime trade is a mainstay of the economy because of the UAE's strategic location on the Persian Gulf, and Dubai's ports at Mina Rashid and Mina Jabal Ali (the largest man-made port in the world) are considered the UAE's premier maritime facilities. The road network is well advanced in urban areas, and a light rail system is under construction in Dubai City. The UAE has six international airports, with a seventh in development, and the planned US$20.4 billion investment in airport infrastructure over the next 20 years could increase passenger traffic exponentially.

Roads: Transport within the UAE is almost entirely road-based. Development of the road network since the 1970s has been rapid, and the quality of the roads is good, particularly in Abu Dhabi and Dubai. The UAE has 1,088 kilometers of paved roadways, including 253 kilometers of expressways. The Dubai Roads and Transport Authority will introduce tolls in July 2007 on its main roadway, Sheikh Zayed Road, and in 2006 began 24 road, bridge, tunnel, and interchange projects in an effort to reduce growing traffic congestion. The Sharjah government also has announced plans to expand the major highways that link Sharjah and Dubai.

In a show of regional unity, and of greater political and diplomatic than economic consequence, the UAE and Qatar have announced they will build a US$1.8 billion causeway linking the two countries. The causeway project will be part of a network that eventually will link four of the six Gulf Cooperation Council states by one road.

Railroads: The UAE currently has no rail network, but construction began in early 2006 on Dubai Metro, a US$4.2 billion, 70-kilometer, two-line urban light rail system. This project, slated to be operational in 2010, will be 100 percent financed by the Dubai Municipality.

Ports: According to the UAE government, 15 commercial ports (including oil terminals) currently serve the country. Located in the city of Dubai, Mina Rashid, completed in 1972, is the leading port of the Gulf region. It has modern facilities to handle almost all types of commercial and passenger shipping, including roll-on-roll-off containers. Also located in Dubai, Mina Jabal Ali, completed in 1979, is the largest port in the country and the largest man-made harbor in the world. It deals primarily in bulk cargo and industrial material for the Mina Jabal Ali Free Zone, an international investment haven.

Dubai Ports (DP) World expects to have the first phase of a multiyear, US$1.5 billion expansion project at Mina Jabal Ali operational in July 2007 and completed in 2008. All phases of the project are slated for completion by 2020. The expansion will increase storage-handling capacity from 7.6 million 20-foot-equivalent units in 2005 and 8.9 million 20-foot-equivalent units in 2006 to 14–15 million 20-foot-equivalent units by 2008. Mina Jabal Ali ranked eighth in the world in terms of total container throughput in 2006.

Mina Zayid, established in 1972, is Abu Dhabi's main general cargo port. Its container terminals handled almost 300,000 20-foot-equivalent units and more than 3.8 million tons of cargo in 2006. Since April 2006, it has been managed by DP World. A 12-year expansion of this port has been underway since 1998. In 2006 the Abu Dhabi government announced plans to build a major new port, Khalifa Port, at Al Taweelah, the first phase of which will cost approximately US$2.2 billion. In 2011, when the first phase is scheduled for completion, operations at Mina Zayid will be relocated to Khalifa Port.

Inland Waterways: The UAE has no waterways of any significant length.

Civil Aviation and Airports: The UAE has 37 airports, 23 of which have paved runways, as well as four heliports. Of the 37 airports, six are international.

Dubai is attempting to become a leading passenger and freight hub by undertaking several major initiatives. Dubai International Airport, which now supports 105 airlines, is undergoing a US$4.1 billion expansion, including the construction of a third passenger terminal by the end of 2007, two new concourses, and a cargo terminal enabling cargo capacity of 3 million tons per year by 2018. In 2005 passenger traffic at the airport reached 24.8 million passengers and in 2006, almost 26 million passengers. This volume is expected to increase to 33 million passengers in 2007 (the UAE government reports a 17 percent increase in passenger traffic in the first quarter 2007). However, projections made by the UAE government of 60 million passengers traveling through the Dubai Airport by 2010 may not be met because Emirates, the state airline, cannot obtain the requisite aircraft. A delivery order for 55 Airbus A380 "superjumbo" airliners has been postponed until late 2008, and options to purchase a fleet of midsized aircraft were cancelled because of manufacturing difficulties. Also under construction is the US$33 billion Dubai World Central International Airport at Mina Jabal Ali, which will have six runways and the capacity to handle 100 million passengers per year.

The newly formed Abu Dhabi Airports Company has embarked on a US$6.8 billion expansion of Abu Dhabi International Airport, including construction of a second runway by March 2008, two new terminals by 2010, a state-of-the-art traffic control complex, and expansion of cargo facilities. Passenger traffic at this airport, which reached 5.5 million passengers in 2005 and 7 million in 2006, is projected to increase to 40 million passengers when the expansion is completed. Al Ayn International Airport, built in 1994, supports 10 airlines, and plans have been made to spend US$20.5 million to expand its facilities. In 2003 Abu Dhabi launched Etihad Airways to compete with Emirates and has invested US$8 billion for 29 new aircraft.

Sharjah International Airport, the first airport to be built in the UAE, launched the low-cost Air Arabia Airlines in 2003 to serve destinations in the Middle East and Asia. Upon completion of a US$61.8 million expansion project in 2007, the airport is projected to have the capacity to handle 8 million passengers per year. Almost 1.5 million passengers traveled through the airport in the first half of 2006.

Pipelines: According to the U.S. government, as of 2006 the UAE had a total of 6,511 kilometers of pipelines. This total includes pipelines designated for various products: condensate, 520 kilometers; gas, 2,580 kilometers; liquid petroleum gas, 300 kilometers; oil, 2950 kilometers; oil/gas/water, 5 kilometers; and refined products, 156 kilometers.

Telecommunications: The US$250 million Dubai Internet City (DIC), opened in 2000, has made Dubai the regional center for e-commerce, attracting major international telecommunications firms. The DIC offers various incentives to companies that locate there, including 100 percent foreign ownership rights, tax-free corporate earnings (guaranteed for 50 years), exemption from customs duties, and full rights to repatriate profits.

Etisalat, the UAE state telecommunications operator, provides Internet access to 1.4 million users and until 2006 had a virtual monopoly on the country's telecommunications; it also operates and maintains the national and international fixed telephone line network, mobile telephony, and cable TV services. The company has been highly successful, has expanded outside the UAE, and has invested heavily in telecommunications infrastructure. To comply with World Trade Organization regulations, in December 2005 a second majority state-owned telecommunications operator, Emirates Company for Integrated Telecommunications (EITC), was established by decree. Operating under the "Du" brand, EITC was scheduled to launch its mobile phone network in 2006, but as a result of technical problems and conflicts with Etisalat, from which it leases bandwidth in rural areas, operations did not begin until February 2007.

In 2004 the UAE government established the Telecommunications Regulatory Authority (TRA) to oversee the general process of telecommunications deregulation. In October 2006, TRA gave Etisalat an official warning for "anti-competitive" activity when it cut prices ahead of Du's launch of mobile phone services.

The UAE is believed to have the best telecommunications network in the Arab World—the highest voice connection and broadband Internet connectivity capacity per capita. The UAE also has the lowest mobile-phone rates in the Arab world (US$0.06 per minute). According to the U.S. government, in 2005 the UAE had more than 4.5 million mobile cellular telephone subscribers, as compared with 1.2 million landlines in use. These numbers represent a penetration rate of, respectively, 101 and 28 lines per 100 residents. The technology used for domestic lines includes microwave radio relay and fiber optic and coaxial cable.

Except for those located in Dubai's Media Free Zone, most television and radio stations are government owned. The government-owned Emirates Media owns Abu Dhabi's radio and television stations. As of 2004, 15 television broadcast stations and 13 AM, 8 FM, and 2 short-wave radio stations were in operation.

GOVERNMENT AND POLITICS

Overview: The UAE is a federation of seven self-governing emirates. The constitution, which was made permanent in 1996, specifies that all powers not specifically allocated to federal institutions remain the prerogative of the individual emirates. In November 2004, Sheikh Zayid ibn Sultan Al Nuhayyan, president of the UAE and ruler of Abu Dhabi since the UAE declared its independence from Britain in 1971, died. In a smooth transition of power, his son, Sheikh Khalifa ibn Zayid Al Nuhayyan, who had been the crown prince of Abu Dhabi for more than 30 years, was named his successor. Sheikh Khalifa's half-brother, Sheikh Mohammed ibn Zayid Al Nuhayyan, succeeded him as crown prince of Abu Dhabi. The ruler of Dubai, Sheikh Maktum ibn Rashid Al Maktum, held the post of prime minister and vice president until his death on January 4, 2006. The following day, the UAE Supreme Council of Rulers named Sheikh Mohammed ibn Rashid Al Maktum, Sheikh Maktum's brother and immediate successor as ruler of Dubai, to be UAE vice president and prime minister. In February 2006, a new Council of Ministers was formed, with various ministries reorganized, several new ministries created, and the second woman cabinet member named. In December 2006, as a first step toward gradual government reform, the first election was held for half the members of the advisory Federal National Council (FNC). The UAE government has indicated support for stronger legal and legislative authority for the FNC.

Abu Dhabi has been historically, and remains today, the politically predominant emirate because of its size, population, oil and gas wealth, portfolio of overseas assets (estimated at US$225–US$250 billion in 2005), and large budget exceeding that of the UAE government. The emirate of Dubai holds a secondary position by virtue of being the hub of private-sector activity. The UAE has neither democratically elected institutions nor political parties.

Constitution: In December 1971, the federation of six Trucial Coast states, later joined by the seventh, agreed on a provisional federal constitution, which was to expire after five years, at which point a formal constitution would be drafted. However, the provisional constitution was renewed periodically until May 1996, when the legislature (Federal National Council) endorsed legislation to make it permanent following approval by the Supreme Council of Rulers (rulers of the seven emirates). In addition to the Federal National Council and the Supreme Council of Rulers, the constitution provides authority for the president and vice president of the union, the cabinet (Council of Ministers), and the federal judiciary and specifies the powers allocated to these institutions. Under the constitution, sharia, Islamic religious law, is a principal source for law. The permanent constitution also names Abu Dhabi as the capital of the state.

Branches of Government: The highest federal authority is the Supreme Council of Rulers, consisting of the rulers of the seven emirates. This body elects the president (who has always been the ruler of Abu Dhabi) and the vice president (who has always been the ruler of Dubai). The president appoints the prime minister and Council of Ministers. The Federal Supreme Council is vested with legislative as well as executive powers. It ratifies federal laws and decrees, plans general policy, and may relieve the prime minister of his post on the recommendation of the president.

The legislature is the Federal National Council (FNC). This body, which under the constitution has responsibility for examining and amending proposed federal legislation, functions only as a consultative assembly. It comprises 40 members appointed by the emirates for a two-year term. The most populous emirates, Abu Dhabi and Dubai, have the most members (eight each); Sharjah and Ras al Khaymah have six members each, and the remaining emirates have four members each. In October 2006, the UAE cabinet approved President Khalifa's proposal to establish an electoral college of notables (selected by rulers and advisers) in each emirate to elect half the members of the FNC; the remaining half were to be appointed. In December 2006, elections were held, at which time the first woman was elected to the FNC; eight women were later appointed.

The federal judiciary encompasses all of the emirates except Dubai and Ras al Khaymah, which have their own local and appellate courts. The UAE has a dual system of sharia courts (administered by each emirate) for criminal and family law matters and secular courts for civil law matters. Sharia courts act in accordance with interpretations of Islamic law but are accountable to the secular Federal Supreme Court. In civil matters, the lowest courts are the courts of first instance, which hear all claims ranging from commercial matters to maritime disputes. Each emirate has a Federal Appeal Court. The highest court of appeal is the Court of Cassation, also known as the Federal Supreme Court; it is located in Abu Dhabi and consists of five judges appointed by the Supreme Council of Rulers. This court is empowered to adjudicate disputes between emirates or between the federal government and individual emirates and to determine the constitutionality of local and federal laws. The emirates of Dubai and Ras al Khaymah do not refer cases to the Federal Supreme Court for judicial review but do maintain liaison with the Ministry of Justice.

The constitution provides for an independent judiciary. However, because judicial decisions are subject to review by the executive branch and justices are predominantly expatriates who can be deported, the U.S. government does not consider the judiciary to be independent. Noncitizen Arabs, who constitute approximately 50 percent of the federal judiciary, serve at the discretion of the government, whereas citizens generally hold permanent judicial positions. Women are barred from serving in the judiciary. The majority of public prosecutors are citizens.

Administrative Divisions: The UAE is a federation of seven emirates—Abu Dhabi (Abu Zaby), Ajman, Al Fujayrah, Dubai (Dubayy), Ras al Khaymah, Sharjah (Ash Shariqah), and Umm al Qaywayn.

Provincial and Local Government: Each of the seven emirates has its own government, which functions in tandem with the federal government. The largest and most populous emirate, Abu Dhabi, has its own central governing body, the Executive Council, chaired by the crown prince; the Eastern and Western Regions and the island of Das are headed by a ruler's representative. Municipalities administer the main cities, each of which has a municipal council. The National Consultative Council functions like the Federal National Council. Local departments carry out various administrative functions. A similar system of municipalities and departments exists in the other emirates.

Judicial and Legal System: Under the UAE's constitution, sharia, Islamic religious law, is a principal source for law. It generally applies to all criminal and family law matters, but in criminal cases the Penal Code may be applied if evidence required by sharia is found to be insufficient. There is no formal system of bail, and defendants have the right to legal counsel only after the police have completed their investigation. Defendants are presumed innocent until proven guilty and have the right to a fair public trial but not necessarily a speedy trial. All trials are conducted before judges rather than juries; trials involving national security (which are heard only by the Federal Supreme Court) and public morality issues are not public. Each court has an appeals process. The military court system is independent of other courts and is used only to try military personnel.

Electoral System: The UAE does not have a system of popular elections; the Federal Supreme Council elects the country's rulers.

Politics and Political Parties: Political parties are prohibited in the UAE.

Mass Media: The government-owned Emirates Media publishes *Al Ittihad* newspaper and owns Abu Dhabi's radio and television stations. Another newspaper, *Al Bayan*, is also government owned, as are most television and radio stations. The country's largest English- and Arabic-language newspapers, *Al Khaleej* and *Gulf News*, are privately owned. By law, the Media Council, which is appointed by the president, licenses all publications and issues press credentials to editors. Laws also govern press content and proscribed subjects. Media Council censors review all imported media for content.

Limits on media freedom are being challenged by the establishment of Dubai Media City (DMC), a free zone intended to attract media and marketing services, business and information services, news media, and multimedia/Internet, as well as publishers, broadcasters, music companies, and production firms. In addition to tax benefits, companies locating there have been guaranteed that the government will not censor their news and information content, provided certain relatively liberal guidelines of taste and propriety are met. In 2006 more than 550 media companies were based at the DMC.

Foreign Relations: In 1981, mainly in response to the threat to regional security posed by the Iran–Iraq War (1980–88), the UAE joined with Saudi Arabia, Kuwait, Bahrain, Qatar, and Oman to form the Cooperation Council for the Arab States of the Gulf, now the Gulf Cooperation Council (GCC). The GCC works to foster greater political, social, and economic integration among Gulf countries and increasingly has focused on improving member states' defense capabilities. The UAE is a member of the United Nations (UN) and the Arab League and has established diplomatic relations with almost 150 countries, including the United States, Japan, China, and most West European countries.

Since 1970, when petroleum exploration began, tensions have existed between the UAE and Iran over the sovereignty of Abu Musa, an island situated between the two countries in the Strait of Hormuz. In 1992, after 20 years of joint control, Iran seized civilian installations on the island and later claimed sovereignty over this island, as well as Greater Tunb and Lesser Tunb. Efforts by the GCC to resolve the dispute failed, and in 1996 Iran opened an airport on Abu Musa and established a power station on Greater Tunb. In December 1999, after numerous attempts to negotiate a settlement through a tripartite committee established by the GCC, the UAE renewed its request for Iran to either enter into direct negotiations or agree to international arbitration. The following year, the UAE stated that it would refer the issue to the GCC committee. In December 2006, GCC leaders reiterated their support for the UAE's sovereignty claim and urged Iran to negotiate a peaceful settlement, possibly with the aid of the International Court of Justice.

In 1990 the UAE opposed Iraq's occupation of Kuwait and provided foreign armed forces opposing the Iraqi invasion with military facilities in the emirates. In 1997, however, the UAE provided humanitarian aid to Iraq, and the following year it expressed opposition to the economic blockade against Iraq and announced that diplomatic ties would be restored. Although the UAE reopened its embassy in the Iraqi capital in April 2000, in that same year it lent support to a GCC declaration that urged Iraq to comply with UN resolutions. This endorsement may have been given to gain GCC support for the UAE in its territorial dispute with Iran. In March 2003, the UAE supported the Arab League resolution pursuant to which member states agreed not to participate in the United States–led campaign in Iraq, but once the conflict began, the UAE agreed to allow U.S. Air Force personnel and combat aircraft to be stationed at Al Dhafra Air Base in Abu Dhabi. The UAE subsequently provided additional humanitarian aid to Iraq and in January 2004 agreed to write off most of Iraq's US$3.8 billion debt.

In response to the attacks of September 11, 2001, the UAE severed diplomatic relations with the Taliban regime in Afghanistan and, together with other GCC members, pledged support for U.S. efforts to bring to justice the perpetrators of the attacks. The UAE did, however, state that it wanted U.S. efforts to be linked to a resumption of the Arab-Israeli peace process. In March 2002, after the defeat of the Taliban and the installation of an interim Afghan government in its place, the UAE reopened its embassy in Kabul. Although the focus of the UAE's foreign policy continues to be Western allies and neighbors, developments in the region, particularly the war in Iraq, the threat of U.S. action against Iran, and U.S. support for Israel during the 2006 conflict with Lebanon remain a serious concern. In January 2007, the UAE pledged US$300 million in loans to Lebanon as part of international efforts to rebuild the country's economy after the summer 2006 war with Israel.

Membership in International Organizations: In 1981 the UAE was a founding member of the Cooperation Council for the Arab States of the Gulf, known today as the Gulf Cooperation Council, or GCC. The UAE is a member of the United Nations (UN) and many of its affiliates and specialized agencies—Food and Agriculture Organization, International Civil Aviation Organization, International Fund for Agricultural Development, International Labour Organization, International Maritime Organization, International Telecommunication Union, UN Conference on Trade and Development, UN Educational, Scientific and Cultural Organization, UN Industrial Development Organization, Universal Postal Union, and World Health Organization. The UAE is also a member of the Arab Bank for Economic Development in Africa, Arab Fund for Economic and Social Development, Arab League, Group of 77, International Atomic Energy Agency, International Bank for Reconstruction and Development, International Criminal Court (signatory), International Criminal Police Organization, International Federation of Red Cross and Red Crescent Societies, International Finance Corporation, International Hydrographic Organization, International Monetary Fund, Multilateral Investment Guarantee Investment Agency, Organisation for the Prohibition of Chemical Weapons, Organization of Arab Petroleum Exporting Countries, Organization of the Islamic Conference, Organization of the Petroleum Exporting Countries, World Intellectual Property Organization, World Meteorological Organization, World Tourism Organization, and World Trade Organization.

Major International Treaties: The UAE is a signatory to various international agreements on aviation, sale of defense articles and services, security of military information, investment guaranties, mapping, postal matters, taxation, and trade in textiles. The UAE is a Non-Annex I country under the United Nations Framework Convention on Climate Change. The UAE is not a signatory to the Kyoto Protocol, but has acceded to it, which has the same legal effect as ratification. The UAE is a signatory to the Nuclear Non-Proliferation Treaty and a party to the

Chemical Weapons Convention; it has signed but not ratified the Biological Weapons Convention. The UAE is also a party to environmental conventions on Biodiversity, Desertification, Endangered Species, Hazardous Wastes, Marine Dumping, and Ozone Layer Protection.

NATIONAL SECURITY

Armed Forces Overview: In May 1976, the UAE's main defense forces were merged, and in November the provisional constitution was amended to give the federal government the exclusive right to levy armed forces and acquire weapons. In 1997 the union was further strengthened when Dubai disbanded its armed forces and integrated them into the federal General Headquarters, which are based in Abu Dhabi. At present, the ruler of Abu Dhabi and UAE president is the supreme commander of the armed forces and as such has strong ties with the United States, which is the UAE's main Western ally. In 2005 the UAE completed a 10-year, US$15 billion program to modernize its armed forces, upgrade its defense capabilities, and acquire modern technology. As a result of these efforts, the country is considered the most rapidly developing military power in the Gulf region. The UAE military consists of an army, navy, and air force. In early 2007, total active troops were estimated at 65,500 personnel: army, 59,000; navy, 2,500; and air force, 4,000.

Foreign Military Relations: The United States remains central to the UAE's defense policy. A defense pact with the United States, negotiated after the 1991 Gulf War and signed in 1996, allows the United States to preposition some troops and equipment in the UAE and affords it some rights to use air bases in the emirates. In 2004 the UAE and the United States signed a US$6.4 billion contract for the delivery of 80 F–16E/F Desert Falcon combat aircraft to the UAE air force by 2007. The first installment, delivered in April 2005, was marked by a high-profile official ceremony. Nearly 1,000 UAE personnel train at U.S. Army aviation centers in the United States. In 2003 the UAE, in conjunction with the United States, Britain, and France, established the Air Warfare Centre at Al Dhafra Air Base to serve as a regional training center, including F–16 training for the UAE and other Gulf Cooperation Council countries. Despite the significance of the military relationship with the United States, the UAE has sought diversification in the procurement of weaponry. France, with whom the UAE has negotiated a defense cooperation agreement, remains a primary source of military matériel, as witness recent purchases of Mirage 2000–9 combat aircraft and Panhard light armored vehicles. Russia, Germany, and Ukraine are also actual or potential suppliers.

External Threats: The UAE is concerned by the military threat posed by Iran, given Iran's unilateral seizure of disputed islands in the Strait of Hormuz, its possession of intermediate-range ballistic missiles, and its suspected development of a nuclear capability. The UAE is not considered to be as vulnerable as Saudi Arabia to the threat from al Qaeda and other militant Islamist groups, as these groups do not have a base of operations or support in the emirates. There are, however, security concerns because of the general volatility of the Gulf region, the repeated terrorist attacks in Iraq, the size and mobility of the UAE's large, predominantly Muslim expatriate population, and the country's alliance with the United States. UAE officials, who meet regularly with their counterparts in the U.S. Departments of State and Defense, are concerned about the deteriorating situation in Iraq, as well as the threat of further U.S. military action in the region, particularly against Iran, and the impact such an action would have on the

UAE's unpopular pro-Western stance. In February 2005, at a major defense conference in Abu Dhabi, the UAE armed forces signed various agreements to purchase satellite surveillance systems and unmanned reconnaissance vehicles. Military experts view this shift away from more traditional military spending as an acknowledgment that the UAE's primary threat is not conventional military attack but rather insurgency and terrorism.

Defense Budget: Defense spending peaked at an estimated US$5.6 billion in 2005 and is estimated to have continued at that level in 2006. The official budget number for 2005 is closer to US$3 billion, but this does not include the significant purchases of military equipment made during the period 1995 to 2005, when the government committed US$15 billion to a rearmament program. It is also likely that additional procurement funds from external state investments are being made available to the military, which further raises the actual level of defense spending well over the official budget number.

Major Military Units: The UAE military is divided into an army, navy, and air force (including a police air wing). The army, which is headquartered in Abu Dhabi, is organized into one Royal Guard brigade, two armored brigades, three mechanized infantry brigades, two infantry brigades, and one artillery brigade (three regiments). Dubai has two mechanized infantry brigades that are not integrated into union forces. The navy is based in Abu Dhabi, with additional facilities in Dubai, Ras al Khaymah, and Sharjah. The navy also includes a marine battalion. Principal air force units include three fighter ground-attack squadrons, one fighter squadron, and one reconnaissance squadron. The air defense force has two brigades (three battalions).

Major Military Equipment: The army's main equipment consists of a combination of primarily French- and U.S.-made armored vehicles. The army is reported to be equipped with 469 main battle tanks, 76 light tanks, 113 reconnaissance vehicles, 430 armored infantry fighting vehicles, 860 armored personnel carriers, 93 towed artillery, 181 self-propelled artillery, 72 multiple rocket launchers, 155 mortars, 6 Scud B (up to 20 missiles) surface-to-surface missiles, 305 antitank guided weapons, 262 recoilless launchers, 62 air defense guns, and 40 surface-to-air missiles. The army's armored capability has been enhanced as part of the UAE's military modernization program. The capability of the newly formed Army Aviation Group will be greatly enhanced by 2010 through a US$300 million helicopter upgrade project.

The navy's inventory includes two frigates, two corvettes, eight missile craft, six coastal patrol craft, five landing craft (tank), and two support and miscellaneous craft. Naval aviation has 11 assault and utility helicopters and another seven helicopters in an antisurface warfare role. As part of its modernization program, the navy is seeking to upgrade blue-water capabilities with the construction of six multirole corvettes and to enhance amphibious capabilities through the acquisition of assault and landing craft as well as amphibious armored personnel carriers for the marine battalion.

The air force has 146 combat aircraft and 40 attack and assault helicopters, as well as assorted reconnaissance, transport, and training aircraft; transport and search-and-rescue helicopters; and both air-to-air and air-to-surface missiles. Air force capabilities are being upgraded significantly through the acquisition of 80 F–16 combat aircraft and 33 multirole Mirage 2000–9 combat aircraft and the upgrading of the 30 Mirage combat aircraft already in the inventory.

Military Service: The UAE's military is an all-volunteer, all-male force, of which an estimated 30 percent are expatriates.

Paramilitary Forces: The UAE's paramilitary force consists of a Coast Guard (under the Ministry of Interior). This force maintains 40 patrol craft (inshore) plus a number of boats.

Foreign Military Forces: The United States negotiated a security agreement with the UAE in 1992 to provide access to UAE air and naval facilities. At Al Dhafra Air Base near Abu Dhabi, the U.S. Air Force's 380th Air Expeditionary Wing has operated aerial refueling tankers, the Global Hawk, and U2 spy planes since early 2002 in support of Operation Enduring Freedom in Iraq. Al Dhafra is expected to become a permanent U.S. air base for regional operations. The United States currently maintains 1,300 military personnel in the UAE.

Military Forces Abroad: In 1984 Gulf Cooperation Council (GCC) members agreed on the creation of a two-brigade (10,000 troops) Peninsula Shield Force, based in Saudi Arabia near the Kuwaiti and Iraqi borders. As of late 2006, the Peninsula Shield Force had 7,000 personnel; it serves as a joint intervention force to defend the joint border of Saudi Arabia, Kuwait, and Iraq. In November 2006, the GCC Joint Defense Council considered a Saudi proposal to expand the capabilities of the Shield and to establish a joint command and control system.

Police: Although the UAE's Ministry of Interior oversees Police General Directorates in each of the seven emirates, each emirate maintains its own police force and supervises its police stations. The strength of the total police force is estimated to be 10,000 personnel. Police stations take complaints from the public, make arrests, and forward all cases to the public prosecutor, who in turn transfers these cases to the courts. In January 2007, the Ministry of Interior announced plans to establish a new crime bureau, with affiliate offices at the individual emirate police departments, to address money laundering, terrorism, and drug trafficking.

Internal Threat: UAE nationals are viewed as generally supportive of the structure of family rule that has defined the UAE's government since independence was declared in 1971. The current president and ruler of Abu Dhabi, Sheikh Khalifa, faces no serious political challenges from within the ruling families of the emirates. Although there are some concerns regarding the politics of the large (80 percent), predominantly Muslim, expatriate population, the loyalty and effectiveness of the government's security forces are considered to be sufficient to meet this potential threat.

Terrorism: In July 2004, the UAE enacted legislation that criminalized the funding of terrorist organizations. The law also increased the amount of time that public prosecutors can hold suspects in terrorism-related cases without charge from 21 days to six months. Terrorism cases are referred to the Federal Supreme Court, which may extend the detention period indefinitely. In February 2006, the UAE passed a cyber crimes law criminalizing the use of the Internet to either promote terrorist ideologies or finance terrorist activities. According to the U.S. Department of State, several meetings of the U.S./UAE Joint Terrorist Finance Coordinating Committee in 2006 resulted in further tightening of the UAE's anti-money laundering laws.

In December 2004, the Dubai Ports Authority (DPA), which operates the main container ports of Mina Jabal Ali and Mina Rashid, became the first Middle Eastern port to participate in the U.S.

Homeland Security Container Security Initiative (CSI) program, which is aimed at preventing materials that could be used by terror groups from entering the United States in shipping containers. Pursuant to the CSI, U.S. customs officers and the Dubai Customs Intelligence Unit jointly screen suspicious United States-bound containerized cargo transiting Dubai's ports.

Dubai is strongly linked to the September 11, 2001, attack on the United States; more than half of the hijackers flew directly out of Dubai International Airport to the United States. In response to concerns that the UAE banking system had been used by the 9/11 hijackers to launder funds, in mid-2002 the UAE adopted legislation giving the Central Bank the power to freeze any suspected accounts for seven days without prior legal permission. In addition, banks have been advised to carefully monitor transactions passing through the UAE from Saudi Arabia and Pakistan and are now subject to more stringent transaction and client reporting requirements.

Human Rights: Although the UAE government has made some advances in the protection of human rights, the U.S. Department of State notes in its annual report on human rights practices that numerous fundamental practices and policies exist to the contrary. Specifically, the UAE does not have democratically elected institutions or political parties; free assembly and association are restricted; and the rights of workers are abused. Trafficking in women and girls, used as prostitutes and domestic servants, and in men, used as servants, laborers, and unskilled workers, continues despite government pledges to end these practices. In July 2005, a federal law was enacted criminalizing the use of persons under age 18 for camel racing. Between late 2005 and early 2006, more than 1,000 children identified by the United Nations and the UAE as trafficking victims were repatriated to their home countries, but according to the U.S. Department of State it is unclear how many underage camel jockeys remain in the country. All Dubai police departments, as well as police departments in other emirates, have human rights and social support offices that furnish assistance to female and child victims of abuse; however, the government is generally viewed as ineffective in protecting women from abuse.

The UAE constitution provides for freedom of speech and the press, but in practice these rights are limited. The government licenses all publications and approves the appointment of editors. Laws also govern press content. Negative comments about Islam, the government, ruling families, or UAE citizens (by expatriates) are punishable by imprisonment, although this regulation is rarely enforced, as the press practices self-censorship. The government restricts access to some Internet sites, and reviews imported printed material for content, imposing distribution limitations on material considered pornographic, excessively violent, derogatory to Islam, or contrary to government foreign policy.

Image courtesy of the CIA World Factbook

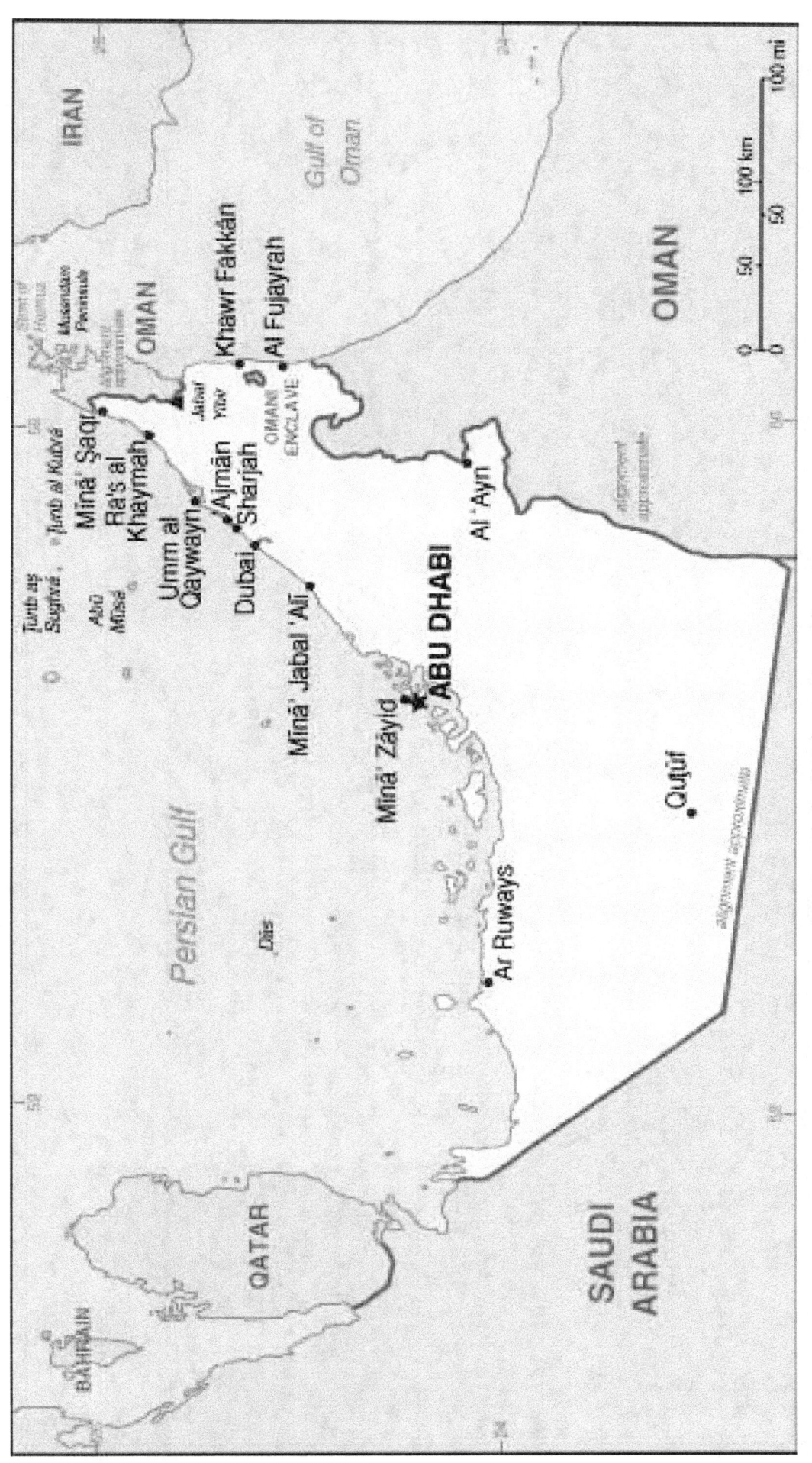

Image courtesy of the CIA World Factbook